CANARIES
AS A NEW PET

Maja Müller-Bierl

CONTENTS

Photography by Horst Bielfeld, Michael De Freitas, Michael Gilroy, Harry V. Lacey, Ron and Val Moat, Mervin F. Roberts.

Distributed in the UNITED STATES by T.F.H. Publications, Inc., One T.F.H. Plaza, Neptune City, NJ 07753; in CANADA to the Pet Trade by H & L Pet Supplies Inc., 27 Kingston Crescent, Kitchener, Ontario N2B 2T6; Rolf C. Hagen Ltd., 3225 Sartelon Street, Montreal 382 Quebec; in CANADA to the Book Trade by Macmillan of Canada (A Division of Canada Publishing Corporation), 164 Commander Boulevard, Agincourt, Ontario M1S 3C7; in ENGLAND by T.F.H. Publications, The Spinney, Parklands, Portsmouth PO7 6AR; in AUSTRALIA AND THE SOUTH PACIFIC by T.F.H. (Australia) Pty. Ltd., Box 149, Brookvale 2100 N.S.W., Australia; in NEW ZEALAND by Ross Haines & Son, Ltd., 82 D Elizabeth Knox Place, Panmure, Auckland, New Zealand; in the PHILIPPINES by Bio-Research, 5 Lippay Street, San Lorenzo Village, Makati, Rizal; in SOUTH AFRICA by Multipet Pty. Ltd., P.O. Box 35347, Northway, 4065, South Africa. Published by T.F.H. Publications, Inc. Manufactured in the United States of America by T.F.H. Publications, Inc.

Origin and History

Bright yellow Border Canary. The Canary has been kept as a pet for thousands of years.

PHYSICAL ATTRIBUTES

Where does he come from? Like all birds, the canary evolved from lizards (flying lizards). He has scales on his legs and feet just like those of a reptile. All other scales have developed into feathers.

Feathers are really no more than elongated scales with fibrous outgrowths along the margins.

Both scales and feathers are

hornlike outgrowths of the skin. Although a feather lacks feeling, like hair or fingernails, it cannot be compared with these items. The feather shaft is hollow at its base so that nutrients may be transmitted during growth. As the feather grows, the shaft is filled with blood. When it is complete, the feather becomes independent of the bird's body; it is "dead" and, unlike hair, is only mechanically attached to the skin.

The Molt: The feather wears out with time; it breaks up or falls out. The canary must completely renew its plumage once a year; this usually occurs from July to September. It starts with the loss of the tail and flight feathers and takes from eight to ten weeks. This is a trying time for the delicate body of the canary, and cock birds will stop singing from time to time. Great care must be taken to ensure that the bird is not injured during the period of feather-growing when the quills are filled with blood. During irregular weather conditions or temperature changes, the molt can begin a second time; this is, of course, unfavorable.

Flying: Most insects fly, as

A pair of Yorkshire Canaries, a Clear Buff and a Variegated (the darker bird).

The Border Canary is one of the varieties that was bred for shape rather than color.

A group of New Color Canaries. The New Color division includes Canaries of many different hues.

do certain mammals (bats), "but the feather is unique," wrote Peterson. "The feather is a wonder of engineering technology. . . . The stiff shaft gives strength where it is necessary, but is bendable at the ends, where pliability is required in fractions of a second for air maneuver. One can feel the smoothness of the vane, soft but tough. One can part the individual barbs and stroke them back together by running them through the fingers, just like a bird would with its beak, as it preens its plumage. Should a bird hit an obstacle, its feathers will part and the barbs will separate. But the bird can soon put his feathers back into order by running his beak along them. If the feathers were composed of a solid piece, this would not be possible; the bird would be left with a permanent split or even a hole in his plumage. With a few such accidents, the bird would no longer be able to fly."

Regular bathing is very important for a canary. For a cage bird, a little bird bath which can be fixed to the cage door is adequate. The bird may not be keen to use the bath immediately; he requires time to get used to it. In the aviary, birds will use open, shallow dishes more readily. The birds' antics, as they carefully clean themselves, are interesting to watch. Their behavior can easily be compared to that of a wild bird.

Body Economy: The feathers are not just to give a bird the power of flight; they are also a form of "air conditioning": they help maintain the body temperature at a constant 40°C (104°F) by forming an insulating layer of air. In warm weather, the air can flow through the feathers. If it is too warm, a bird can cool itself only by bathing or panting, as there are no sweat glands in the skin. A bird should, therefore, never be placed in the full sun or in a heat trap. When it gets colder, the bird can increase the air insulation by expanding its down feathers. On cool evenings, the canary can be compared to a fluffy feather ball as he sits on his perch; to sleep, he puts his head back under his wing and pulls one leg up into his plumage.

A bird cannot fall off his perch when sleeping, as he is attached by the locking mechanism of his toes. When standing or walking, the ligaments in the leg are relaxed; but if he crouches, the ligaments become taut and the toes are locked. The grip can be relaxed only when the bird stands upright.

CLASSIFICATION

The feathers have other important functions; they act as a camouflage suit, as signals for recognition by the opposite sex and, especially, as species characteristics. The science of classification, or taxonomy, endeavors to place all bird species into logical categories by a system of relationships. At

A pair of Canaries. Keep in mind that Canaries are individuals and that no two are exactly alike.

Border Canary.
The bright and
often fluffy
appearance adds
to the Canary's
appeal.

one time, these relationships were based on general characteristics (form, size, feather pattern) but today, behavior analysis also plays a large part. The canary originated from the serin finch and belongs to the: Class: Birds (Aves); Order: Perching Birds (Passeriformes); Family: Finches (Carduelidae); Genus: Serins (*Serinus*); Species: Common Canary (*Serinus canaria*).

The nearest relatives to the Common Canary are the Yellow-crowned Canary *(Serinus canicollis)*, the Citril Finch *(Serinus citrinella)* and the Common Serin *(Serinus serinus)*.

HABITAT

The Yellow-crowned Canary, a near relative of the Common Canary, is found in east and southeast Africa, quite some distance from the Canary Islands, Madeira and the Azores, where the ancestor of our domestic bird is at home. Both habitats are, however, largely agricultural. It was reported from the Canary Islands: "These wild canaries are not just confined to the woods, but they live everywhere there are trees and shrubs. Only in the south of the island, where a desertlike terrain prevails, are they totally absent. Apart from the sparrows, they are the most abundant birds, at least on Tenerife and Las Palmas. . . . The canaries nest, well hidden, in trees, but where the trees are replaced by bush or heathland, as in the higher altitudes, they will also build near the ground." On one of the Azore Islands, ten nests were counted in an area 80 x 40m; they were positioned

Female Dilute Fawn Opal Canary, one of the many New Colors available in today's fancy.

7

1.5–3.5m high in tamarisk trees. The nests were made almost completely from sheep wool.

Mainly domestic canaries were seen in cages on the Canary Islands, but wild birds in cages were no rarity. In Russ's time (1879), wild canaries were rarely imported to Europe. He stated that they were nervous and delicate, and he experienced heavy losses with his imported birds.

The wild canary lives in a moderate climate with a fairly low temperature range. At lower altitudes, the young hatch in March; but at higher altitudes, the birds first begin to build the nest in that month. The hen builds a typical finch nest, mainly from plant fibers. The hen broods alone and is more somberly colored than the cock; matte green, with more gray and less yellow. The cock is mainly green, darker along the back and with a yellow head. The forehead is a most intensive yellow. Russ wrote: "The cock sits near to the hen while she is brooding, preferably high in a leafless tree. . . . From his vantage point he sings loudly and clearly. It is a pleasure to listen to the little virtuoso. . . . How he blows out his throat, how he turns his gold-green shimmering breast, this way and that, so that it catches the native sunlight, until suddenly he hears the quiet call of the hen; then, with his wings drawn in, he skims quietly into the leafy sea of the tree canopy."

Outside the breeding season, wild canaries live together in groups. Their food consists of many carbohydrate and oil-rich seeds, plus much green food. Russ reported that they are fond of figs. The well-known canary seed grows wild in the birds' habitat.

THE DOMESTICATION OF THE CANARY

The canary was first described by Konrad Gesner in 1555. Gesner had not seen the bird himself, but he named it "sugar bird" after the sugar cane

Hybrid Canary; this one is a cross between the Scots Fancy and the Yorkshire.

Border Canary.

Palaces of the Great."

Canaries were probably kept in cages by the Berbers long before the colonization of Madeira (1419) and the Azores (1439) by the Portuguese, and the later conquest of the Canary Islands by the Spanish (1478–1496).

The Portuguese and the Spanish brought the canary back to Europe, where its charming song soon made it a popular cage bird. In the south of Spain, monks began to breed the wild canary in a climate not altogether different from its original habitat. These Spanish monks were, for a long time, the only breeders of canaries, as they ensured that only cock birds were sold. The paying nobility were only interested in good singers; breeding competition was therefore unknown. Eventually, however, the situation changed; somehow canary hens found their way to Italy, where breeding first began in the south, then in the north, and finally in Tyrol (Austria).

At about the same time, the canary spread to other countries, including England, France, and Holland. In England, breeding strategy plantations on the Canary Islands. At this time, few canaries were imported to Europe and, due to their rarity, they were expensive; thus Russ wrote, "to be found only in the changed; more value was placed on the appearance of the birds rather than the quality of their song. The keeping of caged birds was the hobby, even the fashion of the nobility and the rich. Breeding was left to the working classes.

The badly paid mine workers of the Tyrol took to canary breeding as a spare-time occupation, or even full time as

A Non-intensive Orange New Color Canary.

the mining diminished. The Tyrol bird dealers were immortalized in the operetta *Die Vogelhandler* (The Bird Dealers) and in Mozart's *Die Zauberflote* (The Magic Flute). When the bird dealers left on their travels in late summer, it was regarded as a feast day. The men carried as many as 200 birds in little wooden cages affixed to a special carrier on their backs, and wandered for months selling their wares. Some even wandered as far as Russia or Egypt!

The eighteenth century was the heyday of the Tyrol canary breeders; many wandered to the Harz Mountains, where mine workers were required. They took their canaries with them; by now there were yellow, white, and pied varieties. But the quality of the song was the important thing for the Tyrolers. For a time, they even kept nightingales to teach the young cock canaries to sing.

In the Harz

Scots Fancy Canary. Members of this variety are also called Scotch Fancies.

Mountains, even greater value was placed on the quality of the song; the best singers brought the best prices. There were even "umpires" who placed values on individual birds. From 1842, transport began to the Americas, and in the second half of the nineteenth century, the "Harzer Roller" stud was established.

Even before the arrival of canaries in the Harz, a great tradition of bird trading existed, with dead birds as well as living ones. Bird catching was a common pastime. For the transport of birds, the so-called "Harzer Bauer" (Harz cage) was developed. These wooden cages were manufactured in the home with the help of the whole family and, in some cases, became a source of additional income.

In the nineteenth century, canary breeding spread to every part of the Harz Mountains. Even though people were cramped for room in their little houses, they always found space for canary breeding. In the summer, the excess hens were disposed of; at the end of October or beginning of November, the young cocks and sorted adults. The dealers

bought up the birds and packed them into their "Harzer Bauer," placed 160 or 170 of them onto a light carrying frame, and covered the lot with linen. The transport to Luebeck took about twelve days. The march was strenuous, as the load measured 1.5m high, .78m wide and .63m thick. After each league (4.6 miles), the birds were fed; every three days the cages were cleaned out. "In spite of this tedious form of transport," wrote Reiche (*Gefiederte Welt* 1/82), "the heavily laden carriers strode cheerfully and happily on their way,

A quartet of Canaries. Note the bright red color of the middle two birds.

accompanied at every stride by the warbling song of a hundred avian vocal cords. Attracted by the far-reaching melodies, free-living relatives of the canaries came in flocks; finches, linnets, and the like, apparently amazed at this caravan, accompanied the column for long distances."

The same animal merchant, Reiche, organized the first canary transport to America in

1842. The crossing by sailing ship took months. As canary keeping was unknown there, it was not easy for him to find buyers for his thousands of birds. However, in only a few years the hobby became just as popular as in Europe. Reiche reported "In 1853 we turned over 10,000 birds; in 1860,

Northern Dutch Frill Canary. Note the swirling plumage on this bird.

15,000."

Through the advent of the railways and steamship transport, the canary trade further increased. From July, 1882 to April, 1883, Reiche transported 120 thousand canaries to New York. Each year he exported 10,000–12,000 cock birds to South America. In 1893, it is estimated that 300 thousand canaries were bred; in Andreasberg alone, 30,000–40,000 cocks. With the improvement of postal services, a mail order scheme evolved; this was the end of the travelling dealers.

A large amount of literature evolved, and in 1879, there were twenty specialist journals. Canary societies formed in 1870.

In some of the early documents, it was often reported that women played a major part in the success of breeding programs. An 1889 issue of *Gefiederte Welt* (Feathered World) states: "Herr Painter/Decorator E. Hinze and his wife of Berlin who visited Trute " (a well-known Roller canary breeder, a miner from St. Andreasberg), and at first found it difficult to enter, were

German Crested Canary and a hybrid: Black-headed Canary (*Serinus alario*), Common Canary cross.

impressed with the care and cleanliness in the breeding stud and noted that Frau Trute was as much involved with the birds as was her husband. The clerk of court, Wilhelm Bocker from Wetzlar, writer of many papers on canary breeding, found it noteworthy that the wives of breeders in the Harz were just as busy with the birds and as knowledgeable as the men.

Naturally, the canary fancy also had its swindlers. It was reported in 1893: "When the dealer takes his wares in big flight cages and wanders from house to house accepting part-payments, one can be sure that birds which he has bartered or mistakenly included during sorting, are contained with the cock birds." So there were dealers who sold old cock birds and young hens as young cocks, while the actual singers commanded higher prices. In some places, such swindles were big business. In St. Petersburg, Reiche reports that "markets dealt in bad stock; indeed, thousands of hens are dishonestly passed off as cocks, a practice which is undermining the fancy."

After the First World War, canaries were still bred in massive quantities. K. Neunzig wrote in 1926: "In some of these breeding establishments, a minimum of 400–500 cock birds are produced each year; whether this is an ideal situation can only be speculated upon." In 1926, nearly half a million German canaries were exported to America. The mass transport ended with the outbreak of World War II. Today, only a few remnants of the Harz Canary Guild carry on their trade. After the war, birds could be bred only with the greatest of difficulties, often with American help. General Clay wanted to acquire two genuine Harzer Rollers and visited a St. Andreasberg breeder. Thereafter, the difficult postwar

Border Canary. This variety comes in many different colors.

time for breeders was somewhat relieved!

The mass dealing in canaries, as one can see, is at an end. The most important role is now played by the societies, where breeding is regarded as a hobby. Of course, the "black sheep" and the swindlers have not died out. It is good, therefore, when a prospective purchaser finds a dealer or breeder whose expert opinion can be trusted. This does not mean, however, that a breeder can never make a mistake in sexing birds.

New Color Canaries, a cinnamon and an orange.

Acquisition and Accommodation

Hybrid Fife Fancy Canary.

CHOOSING A BIRD

If you require a singing canary, then you should choose a cock bird. As different birds have varying singing abilities, it is wise to give yourself time to listen to the songs of various birds. Perhaps one likes a loud, warbling song; those with sensitive hearing will prefer a bird with softer voice. It must be considered that a loud singing bird is not particularly suitable for an echoing apartment.

Canaries are not necessarily kept just for the pleasure of hearing their song. There are canaries with attractive appearances— either with beautiful plumage or exciting stature. The latter include the Border Canary or the crested forms.

When breeders cannot sell their excess hens, they are in a difficult situation.

That was the case in the nineteenth century. Russ (1888) wrote: "Reiche gives the advice that, as unnecessary consumers of food, many excess females should be culled from the nest. I will neither agree nor disagree with that advice, but Reiche finds this better than foregoing the unpleasant duty, and releasing numerous hens in the most breeders do not have such problems.

If you decide to acquire one or more canaries, you are taking on a big responsibility. With careful care, a canary can live for ten to fifteen years. During vacation periods, you must find a place where your bird will be properly cared for, perhaps with a neighbor or in a pet shop. You

Border Canary and Lizard Canary. The "Lizard" is the bird with the plumage that looks like scales.

fall to an uncertain fate, or worse, to place the unwanted hens in substandard accommodation in the attic and, through meanness, to deny them a proper diet." As can be seen, one-sided wishes of purchasers can lead to an unhappy fate for excess hens. Today, fortunately, must prepare yourself to contend with bird "trademarks," such as feathers or seed husks on the carpet. Many cage birds die much too young from diseases, most of which could have been cured if their keeper had consulted a veterinarian early enough.

The best time to obtain a canary is in the late fall, November or December; by this time, the young canaries of the season will have completed their first molt. At this time, the breeders dispose of their excess stock and there is a greater choice of birds. Of course, this is just before the Christmas holiday and the problems of birds on the Christmas tree are well known. You may therefore elect to choose a less hectic time to purchase your pet,

Gold Lizard Canary with a broken, or clear, cap.

perhaps foregoing your plans for a vacation. Canaries can be obtained most times of the year.

Distinguishing the sexes can be difficult in canaries. The most obvious indication is the song, which is performed mostly by cock birds. The expert can distinguish the sex of a bird by examining the cloaca where, in the cock bird, there is is said that a cock will sing less often if he has a mate, but if the cage is large enough, the opposite can prevail. One should never place two cocks together in a small cage.

The physical condition of a bird is an important consideration when you are buying. If a cock is singing, it is a good indication that it is

A Red-orange New Color Canary.

a puckering of the skin when he is in breeding condition. In addition, the eyes of a cock bird are more vivid.

It is perhaps nicer to obtain a pair of pet birds, providing they can get along with each other. It happy and healthy. This does not necessarily mean, however, that a cock bird is sick if he is not singing in the dealer's premises; perhaps he does not like the position in which his cage has been placed. It is important that the plumage is smooth and tight, with no bald patches. The legs should be smooth and clean. Canaries are lively birds, constantly on the move and hopping from perch to perch. Soiled feathers around the vent, a lack of liveliness, and sitting quietly with the plumage fluffed out with half-closed eyes are warning signs that the bird is sick. The move from premises to premises and strange surroundings can be a most stressful time for a bird, resulting in sickness which should, of course, be treated. The molt is also an unpleasant and stressful time, but it is not a sickness.

CAGES AND THEIR FURNISHINGS

The domestic canary is no longer as delicate as its wild ancestors. In 1879, Russ wrote about wild canaries: "They are nervous birds, which take a long time to lose their inherited wildness and are prone to

A pair of Border Canaries, a Variegated Yellow male and a Variegated Cinnamon female.

quickly damage their plumage in the confines of a cage. . . . There can hardly be a more delicate seedeater; most are lost through fits or convulsions." This great bird man, although much of his work is now outdated, had formulated a hundred years ago avicultural ideas which would put even recent developments to shame. "The biggest shame," wrote Russ in 1888, "is that nearly everyone keeps their birds in cages much too small. Some young canaries are kept for far too long in the Harzer cages, with the tiniest amount of space. That such a cultured masterpiece as the canary can withstand these indignities is amazing; but can natural development take place? . . . but, should all kinds of deformities develop over a short or long time, one can really blame it on the tiny cage . . . while the bird is destined to become a martyr." Russ continued: "As a rule, one should take the opinion that a cage, for whatever kind of bird, can never be too large." He warned about round "tower cages," in which birds could develop the "turn sickness." Round cages are really

unsuitable for canaries; even large flight cages, in the round form, take up too much unnecessary space.

In 1888, Russ complained that too many unsuitable cages were offered on the market: "They should mend their old humdrum ways and, instead of the fashionable round and other unsuitable cages, should buy sensible cages at the outset." And he complained: "They regard these 'martyr boxes' as splendid luxury cages, fashioned in brass, bronze, polished wood, and so on; often

Dark Yellow male and Clear Buff female Border Canaries.

in round, hexagonal, or octagonal form; decorated with various ornaments, balconies, ladders, flags and other embellishments (or, more appropriately, disfigurements). . . . I cannot regard such things as attractive; they are, to say the least, superfluous. There is hardly room in these alcoves and balconies for a little bird to find a cozy corner. The cage takes up too much space, appears much larger than it really is and costs too much."

Embellished cages, pagodas, and so on should not be regarded as nostalgic homes for our birds. A hundred years ago they were already recognized as absurd and useless, perhaps best used for an artificial bird. Anyone with a predisposition to nostalgia can find other things from early aviculture to satisfy his whims, indeed to the benefit of the birds. I am thinking especially of the readiness of many people to provide this or that bird with relatively spacious living accommodations and to provide natural perches of branches and twigs; perhaps even to build a cage oneself.

It is no longer difficult to find a suitable home for our feathered friends, one which is compatible with our knowledge

of modern veterinary medicine and aviculture. Basically, a cage should not be tower-shaped, as a canary is not a climbing bird. Passerine birds, such as the canary, hop from twig to twig and fly a lot. A canary cage should preferably be longer than its height. "A distance of 40 cm. between perches is necessary for a canary to perform several wing beats," says a well-known veterinarian. The perches must be at least 10 cm. from the cage walls. The minimum width of a cage should be 30 cm., as the canary's wingspan is 24 cm. The cage should also have adequate height, so that the bird is confined not only to horizontal movements but, as a knowledgeable aviculturist recommends, also to vertical ones so that "intensive and changing muscle action" is encouraged. This, of course, means having perches at several levels; and the height of the cage should be at least 45 cm. Anyone who does not have the space to keep a cage at least 60 x 30 x 45 cm. should allow his bird plenty of free flight. In any case, choose a cage which is easy to clean and does not contain nooks and crannies where mites and the like can

Border Canary. Your pet's cage must be big enough to provide the bird with ample opportunity for movement and exercise.

hide.

A metal cage is fundamentally easier to disinfect than a wooden one. However, the so-called wooden box cages (sides and back wooden, only the front of wire) have always been popular. They offer protection from drafts and give the birds a feeling of security. They must, however, be regularly painted. The handy person can easily construct such cages himself. One can also give wire cages a "box character" by affixing suitably sized sheets of hardboard to the sides and back. This is especially recommended if you want to protect your wallpaper and furniture from bird droppings.

OUTDOOR AVIARIES AND THEIR FURNISHINGS

Anyone who considers building an outside aviary himself is recommended to read the book *Aviaries: A Complete Introduction* (TFH Publications). It is also possible to purchase aviary panels, which can be easily assembled. The main advantage

of an outdoor aviary is that the birds can live in more natural conditions than are possible indoors. If the aviary is not overpopulated with birds, it may be planted with suitable shrubs, such as black elder (*Sambucus nigra*, not the poisonous grape elder!), laurel, hawthorn, weeping pine, dwarf pine, stone pine, giant thistle, and mullein. If these are planted directly in the aviary, it becomes more difficult to fulfill the demands of hygiene. If the aviary floor is concrete, plants in tubs may be used.

One must ensure that there are enough perches, feeding pots, and roosting sites; otherwise, certain birds will suffer. It is wise to keep an eye on the birds when they go to roost, and also after feeding. Be sure that perches are not set over food and water vessels.

HYGIENE AND HEALTH

Here we will only briefly cover the most important points. The site of the cage or the aviary should be well ventilated, but free of drafts. The birds should have access to sunlight but, at the same time, must be able to seek out the shade. A regular bath is important for canaries. If you do not have a roof cover on your outdoor aviary, it will be more natural, but more dangerous for the birds.

Regular cleaning and occasional disinfecting of the accommodation, the perches, the food and water dishes are important. Drinking water must be renewed daily, after the vessel has been cleaned. Bath water may be used for drinking—a bird will not bathe in dirty water, but he will drink it! The canary needs light and air; it can withstand the cold, but not damp cold. A canary should never be moved from a warm room into the cold. During the molt, a canary should not be moved at all.

One of the most common problems of canaries is the red

A Lizard Canary taking a bath. Your Canary's cage should be equipped with some sort of "bathtub."

mite. These can be exterminated; pet shops supply suitable remedies. If the claws are inadequately exercised because of unsuitable perches, they will grow too long and must be trimmed.

Yellow Frosted New Color Canary. The term Frosted describes plumage which has no color on the tips of the long feathers.

Canaries as Companions

WHY AND HOW THE CANARY SINGS

The canary is a songbird.

Many fanciers value the Canary for its famous song as well as for its looks.

and variety of tones; the longer segments may be regarded as verses." As the single sounds mainly consist of several layered tones, the hen is able to localize the sound; this means the sound does not just attract the hen, she is able to find the position of the singing cock. "What first appears to be a luxury, a loving song, is really an absolute necessity." At the same time, the song

Bird song has been defined as follows: "The song differs from the call in the richness

As you can see, Canaries come in many styles. Choose the bird whose appearance and vocal talents most appeal to you.

is a species recognition signal and a territorial sign to rival cocks. Peterson, an experienced aviculturist, writes: "Romantics, who believe bird song to be a jubilant expression of the joy of life, find it difficult to believe that it is much more a territorial claim against rivals. The song becomes more frequent and aggressive when another cock is within hearing distance. If an intruder should cross the invisible demarcation line of a territory, he will be attacked."

Through the centuries of captive breeding, the song of the domestic canary has changed from that of its wild ancestor. Experiments reveal the typical song of a domestic canary to consist of recognizable stanza structures (generally known as "tours"), while those of the wild canary consist of barely recognizable single tones. The stanzas of a wild canary are short. However, the basic structures of the songs are surprisingly similar.

The Harzer Roller Canary has four main kinds of tour: the hollow roll, the bass, the hollow bell, and the flute; then, in addition, the bell, the water tour, the schockel, and the glucke. The Belgian Canary has an even greater repertoire of song which has been described as "hiccuping." The bird does

not always sing with a closed beak, as does the Harzer Roller.

What are described as "defective tours" by breeders may be attractive to the layman. I have known canary keepers who have found the loud song of a bird with open beak much more agreeable than the soft sounds emitted from a bird with closed beak. Anyone desiring a singing bird should acquire one to his own taste, which will depend on the capacity of his nerves and the tolerance of his neighbors!

FEEDING

If you have only a few birds, commercial canary mixtures are recommended, those which carry the date of manufacture. The keeping guarantee is valid only when the seed is properly stored (usually for twelve months): dry (the relative humidity under 70%), cool (about 10°C or 50°F), and dark. It is best to purchase small quantities from clean and efficient stores. The mixtures consist of oil-rich seeds (rape, niger, hemp, linseed, poppy and lettuce seed) and carbohydrate-rich seeds (canary seed, millet, oats).

It is not necessary to throw uneaten seeds away every day, but the empty husks should be blown off before the feeding dish is refilled, enough to last the bird to the next feeding. A

A trio of Canaries. If you plan to keep more than one songbird, be sure their cage or aviary is very roomy or, safer yet, keep them in separate accommodations.

kept in a heated room. A bird which flies a lot will require more food than one sitting in a small cage.

The canary, like all of his relations, does not survive on seed alone, he also requires green food, which is very healthy for him. For calcium and mineral requirements, a cuttlefish bone will suffice; this will also be used to keep the beak in trim. Bird sand should be sprinkled on the cage floor; this usually contains calcium and minerals. Bird grit should also be made available. During the molt, a vitamin supplement should be given (obtainable from pet stores), especially when no green food is available.

full dish does not necessarily mean that the bird is well kept; the keeper may have overlooked the husks covering the seeds; many a bird has starved when having an apparently full food dish. If a canary is allowed to eat too much of its favorite food (usually hemp), it will get too fat and prone to sickness. Obese cock canaries will no longer sing. Naturally, one should not wait until the food dish is totally empty before refilling it. The quality of the seeds is variable, and a bird should not be forced to eat seeds which he does not like or are even bad. The amount of food a canary eats varies. A bird which is kept outside in the winter will require more calories than one

A pair of Border Canaries. If you keep more than one Canary, be sure there is ample food for each bird.

Now and again, a little powdered charcoal may be given. This may be strewn over the clean bird sand or in the feeding dish.

Pet stores offer a variety of canary tidbits; these should be given sparingly; otherwise the birds will become too fat. Canaries are especially fond of pieces of apple or some grated carrot. Allow the birds to get accustomed to items they do not recognize; this may take a little time.

TAMING AND FREE FLYING

Do not expect a newly-acquired bird to sit immediately on your finger or shoulder. A bird is not necessarily tame because it has been bred in captivity. One should not expect too much from a tame canary. There are some parrot species which love to be taken in the hand and petted, especially when they are young. If you want a pet to stroke, you should not choose a bird but rather an animal like a guinea pig. A canary does not learn to talk like a budgerigar; it does not like to be cuddled like some big, tame parrots. It has other attributes: it has a cheerful manner, it sings, it has an ornamental appearance and is always on the move. When hopping and flying, he can almost turn on the spot, but this can only be seen in a large flight. The "triple hop" arrangement of three perches will encourage the canary to sing and hop from perch to perch in a somewhat monotonous manner, something which may get on the nerves of some people.

Free flight cannot outweigh the advantages of a flight cage. A bird is much safer in a flight cage, protected from the dangers of the room (poisonous plants like sanseveria, African

Opposite: A Fawn Border Canary. *This page:* A pair of New Color Canaries. Proper perches are essential for the well-being of your pet or pets. Safe natural branches are ideal for this purpose.

violets, etc., which he might peck at, hot electrical appliances, ovens, etc., on which he could land). Even when you think you have removed all hazards, there is always the danger of the unexpected. Large mirrors and crystal clear windows are a particular hazard; you cannot regard the bird as stupid if it flies into one of these and breaks its neck—it cannot see the glass. Indeed,

A White Variegated male Border Canary.

many people have collided with a glass door! If a canary should escape through an open window, his conspicuous colors might soon make him a victim of an attack from a bird of prey or a cat. If he escapes in the cold, damp months, his days will be numbered.

Before a bird is allowed free flight in a room, he must at least be tame enough to trust people, as panicked flying can be particularly dangerous. It is convenient when the bird is prepared to sit on an outstretched finger or on your shoulder. A canary can really develop a close relationship with his keeper (as is the case with other song birds), provided the keeper has a gentle and understanding manner and is careful even in the way he dresses (nothing to shock the bird!). Naturally, these things take time; patience and feeling are essential. Nothing can be achieved by force. It would be quite wrong, for example, to place a newly acquired canary in the center of the room and surround him with friends and relatives. Even if they all speak to him, whistle at him, and offer him tidbits, the bird will not recognize their good intentions;

Consult your pet shop for the proper way to handle your pet Canary before attempting to hold it in any way. Canaries are delicate birds that must be handled gently.

he will be more likely to feel threatened.

The first sign of trust offered by a canary is when he stays in position when his keeper approaches. Later, he will come to accept tidbits from the hand. Finally, a bird should not be forced to learn through starvation; it is enough to remove his favorite treat (hemp, for example), and offer this from your hand.

When the canary is to return to his cage, his feed dish (which should be plainly visible to him) should be freshly filled, or tidbits should be placed in the cage. This will not work, of course, if the bird has been fed just before leaving the cage, or worse, has eaten during his free flying. The inside of the cage should be the only feeding place. The larger the cage, and the better it is fitted out to the bird's liking, the more readily he will return.

When the bird is free flying in a room, the principles of hygiene should be observed. A bird will defecate wherever he happens to be. Therefore, it is necessary to keep an eye on him. He should not sit on your head, and, on no account, should he be allowed on the dinner table.

COMMUNITY

Tame canaries are less common than tame budgerigars, and such contacts as seen between parrots and their owners are out of the question. The canary does not have such a close bond with his own kind as, for example, lovebirds do. The canary is, however, not a solitary bird. Outside the breeding season, wild canaries live together in large flocks. They pair up only in the breeding season, as is the case with many bird species, and protect their territories against other members of their own species. If you think about the meaning of the song, you understand that the canary cock urgently requires a mate. There are bird species in which the cock abandons the brooding hen, who must then raise the brood by herself (weaver birds, for example). However, with canaries, the cock takes part in rearing the young. Canaries are, therefore, naturally social with their own kind, with the mate during the breeding season, and in flocks outside of it.

A mirror, as a substitute for a

An Apricot Red Factor Canary. A good Red Factor is hard to find and is therefore an expensive bird.

mate, is much less appropriate for a canary than for a budgerigar (a cock budgerigar would even accept a male partner). The cock canary would regard his image as a rival and attack, or would possibly be afraid of it; both possibilities would, over a period, be unhealthy for him. He may peck at the mirror, as he would many things, out of curiosity. A mirror will not necessarily make him sing more; in fact, the opposite may occur.

If you have two canaries and want them to sing, you must keep them in such a way that they can hear each other but cannot see each other. It is no good to place one cage on top of the other, as the canaries will just sit on the wire and attempt, by various contortions of the body, to see each other. If they should be successful, they will repeat it time and time again. This is not a useful achievement! It is difficult to judge how these "song battles" will eventually affect the health of the participants. As an example, I remember, many years ago, when I had two cock canaries in one cage above the other. One day, when I opened

the doors of both cages to allow the birds free-flight, the red bird made its way immediately into the other cage and attempted to drive the yellow one out. Later, the yellow bird developed a bad habit which often occurs with singly kept canaries: eating its own droppings (this is probably a behavioral disturbance).

It is quite clear that two cocks should never be kept together in a small cage; they would rarely get on with each other. Of course, it is possible to keep a community of several canaries of both sexes, when the accommodation is of sufficient size. It is difficult to assess how much space is required for each

Never keep two male Canaries together in a cage, no matter how docile they may seem to you.

bird. Too many factors (shape, position, height of the accommodation and its surroundings) are involved; in addition, each bird is in itself an individual. Spare quarters should always be available for emergencies.

A good possibility is to keep a pair of canaries which are compatible with each other (cock and hen are not necessarily compatible when introduced). At the moment, I keep a pair of canaries and a pair of Zebra Finches together in a large cage in front of a window. The lively Zebra Finches add movement, but canaries are also naturally lively birds; they hop and fly very well, moving about for most of the day. The cock canary, in particular, sings a lot.

At first, I kept the two pairs in a cage 60 x 40 x 50 cm. In flight, the birds occasionally had a slight collision and, as there was insufficient feeding area, the Zebra Finches tended to be pushed out. The situation soon changed when I placed the birds in a larger flight cage (80 x 40 x 100 cm.). The little Zebra Finches then became more than a match for the

Opposite: A lovely Yorkshire Canary. *This page:* Gloster Fancy Canary. Note the characteristic "corona" or crest on this bird.

relatively large canaries. In the larger cage, the cock Zebra Finch came into breeding condition; the little fellow chased the canaries from his "tree" (a bunch of twigs bound to the back of the cage), tried to pull the smaller twigs off and began to pull on the tail feathers of his mate. In order to satisfy his nest building instinct, he had to be busy with something. A bunch of raffia gave him something which he could carry up into the twigs (even though it could never become a nest). He hung the strands in the twigs and became so busy that he often did not even notice when the canaries also had a go. The canaries moved not only in the upper part of the cage but also in the middle and lower levels, where the feeding areas were. At night, they roosted on their swing. When a pair get on well with each other, it is not unusual to see them, at night, sitting close to each other on a perch.

Although the Zebra Finch, with his speed, is a match for the canary, the canary cock can protect himself. He looks in the direction of his opponent, opens his beak and, with loud voice and fluttering wings, makes an impressive display. The hen can do it almost as well and drives away the cock with threatening

This page: A trio of Border Canaries. *Opposite:* A pair of New Color Canaries.

gestures. Whoever is the most aggressive at a particular time is the winner. The arguments are mostly over feeding or nesting sites. The jealousy over food can work out favorably: with my singly kept canaries, I never witnessed such an attack on a cuttlefish bone as I did in the community cage. The canaries were excited by the Zebra Finches pecking at it, and vice versa. One must take the view that this type of excitement is healthy, as opposed to the stressful permanent suppression or tyrannization which can occur in different circumstances. One must always be ready for

emergencies—to remove the aggressor or to save the oppressed, whatever may be the case.

Other songbirds (especially tits) frequently visit the balcony outside the window, perhaps attracted by the birds or the millet sprays attached to the cage roof. The canaries were quite happy in their window cage, nosily observing what was going on outside.

For a mixed community cage with canaries, many other kinds of finches are ideal, excepting the more aggressive species. Diamond Doves or Chinese Painted Quails may be acquired if the minimum floor area is one square meter. For ease of feeding, only smaller seedeaters should be kept together. Budgerigars are not suitable, as they are climbing birds, and the cage should be prepared more for hopping than climbing. In a very large aviary, particularly an outdoor aviary, a more substantial mixture of inmates is possible. But beware of overcrowding; this can result in injuries and deaths; in addition, overcrowding can lead to infectious diseases spreading through the stock very quickly.

Border Canary.

Canary Reproduction

A pair of Gloster Canaries, a crested and an uncrested.

FEEDING

During the breeding season, canaries must have supplements in addition to their basic diet. The wild canary changes its diet from season to season. Wild canaries, like their domestic cousins, are fond of half-ripe seeds from various grasses.

They like to nibble at tender buds and shoots, they love fruit, especially figs, and they also eat wild herbs.

Of the "local weeds," our canaries prefer chickweed,

dandelion leaves, half-ripe dandelion heads, shepherd's purse, thistle, plantain, and half-ripe seeding grasses. Green food is very important during brooding, but there is a danger of diarrhea if too much is given. Be sure not to give green food which has been treated with chemicals, and do not collect it from road verges where vehicle pollution is likely.

Soaked seed, in particular rape, canary seed and whole oats, is vitamin rich and easily digested. First wash the seed and place it in a shallow (approximately 3 cm.) dish;

cover it with water and place it in a warm site. Leave it for twelve to twenty-four hours (depending on the room temperature), then drain. To prevent souring or molding (especially in the warmer months), the seed should be washed several times a day in a strong current of water. The soaked seed is most valuable when it just begins to sprout.

For rearing the chicks, canaries need egg food. Special egg biscuit is available on the market (you can also bake this yourself, but without baking powder) as well as various

A Norwich Canary and a Gloster Canary. It is likely that one of the Norwich's ancestors was the Lizard Canary.

rearing foods. Experienced breeders often develop their own recipes. A particularly valuable supplement has been developed by an experienced aviculturist which gives to seedeaters the fats and animal proteins which may be lacking in their normal diet. Dietary supplements can be obtained from your local pet shop where the dealer will be pleased to offer you the benefits of his valuable experience. These supplements are also valuable during the molt.

BREEDING PROCESS

One must, of course, give a pair of canaries time to become accustomed to each other. If they squabble a lot, this is not an indication that they are incompatible. Antipathy occurs sometimes only through fear. This can sometimes be alleviated by supplying more feeding dishes, more cuttlefish bones, and more than one bath, thus doing away with the rivalry over feeding. Then, if the cage is sufficiently large, two apparently incompatible birds will perhaps become a harmonious pair.

A nest pan must be provided for the hen. This is best hung in the upper part of the cage. Nest pans made from wire or earthenware are available. Nest material consists of hard and soft fibers; the former include sisal, coconut fibers and dried grasses. Soft fibers are used to line the nest. The reproductive behavior of canaries is complicated.

All sexual acts, external influences, and hormonal stimulants are not only intertwined with each other; they also have several effects. As the hours of daylight increase, the pituitary gland releases hormones which stimulate the ovary to produce estrogen, the sex hormone. Under the effects of estrogen, the hen reacts positively to the advances of the cock. Mating will then occur. It is not only the longer days which bring the

There are several types of frilled Canaries; a few are the Gibber Italicus, the Parisian Frill, and the Northern and Southern Dutch Frills.

A Fife Fancy Canary and a Border Canary (the lighter bird).

hen into breeding condition, but also the advances of the cock, particularly with regard to his song. Under the influence of estrogen, the hen builds her nest. This excites her even more, and the secondary hormones come into action. Progesterone ensures that the eggs are developed and laid; prolactin causes the hen's breast feathers to fall out, making her breast more sensitive to the feel of the eggs, and allowing her to warm them more efficiently. Due to this sensitivity of the breast, the hen stops using hard fibers in the nest building and uses feathers instead. Through the excitement of nest building and laying, enough prolactin is produced to dull the effects of the estrogen. The sexual drive is thus diminished, allowing the hen to devote all her time to brooding and rearing the clutch.

The gonads of male songbirds are also activated in the spring. If the pair should mate too early, there is a possibility that eggs will be infertile. It has been stated: "It is wrong to feed the birds in winter with miserly or cheap foods as some breeders still do. At one time, the general opinion was that, as the birds had little to do in the winter (no breeding, no molting, no showing), it was not necessary to give them a full diet. Furthermore, it was thought that a diet of rape seed would hinder a premature breeding instinct. . . . A balanced, varied diet in the winter will ensure that the birds are fit and strong for the breeding season."

Signs that the cock bird is in breeding condition include increased and more passionate singing. The hen will show a nervous disposition: she will fly backwards and forwards, answering with her trilling call-note. When ready to mate, she will crouch on the perch and raise her tail. Mating behavior includes the feeding of the hen by the cock.

The hen shapes the nest interior with turning movements of her body. Between five and ten days after the first mating, the first egg is laid. A clutch consists of three to six eggs. One is laid each day, usually early in the morning. While the hen is laying, the birds require complete peace and quiet and should on no account be disturbed. When the hen leaves the nest, one can gently remove the egg and replace it with a dummy egg. It is recommended that the egg be carefully removed with a teaspoon, then laid on wadding or lint. It is best to place them into a cigar box which has been divided into small compartments with cardboard. Each compartment is given a number, so that the eggs do not become mixed up.

This measure is necessary so that the young hatch at about the same time. The wild canary does not brood the first egg, but starts at the one before last. Over the years, the domestic canary has changed its brooding habits and will start early brooding. This results in some chicks hatching days before the others, giving them a mixed chance of survival—the strongest (and oldest) chicks will receive most of the food.

The hen broods alone but is

A Border Canary.

53

fed by the cock. She leaves the nest only to defecate. The chicks hatch in thirteen to fourteen days. Both parents take part in feeding the youngsters but, in the early days, only the hen will feed them as she continues to be fed by the cock. In the first week, the droppings of the chicks are contained in a membrane, and these droppings are removed from the nest by the hen. Later, the chicks are strong enough to defecate from the nest; the membrane is no longer necessary. Week-old chicks appear somewhat "prickly," but in ten to twelve days, the quills open up and they then look like little balls of fluff.

Fledging is a time of great excitement. The youngsters must learn to estimate distances and target their landings. They soon begin to feed themselves, but will continue to be fed by the parents, mainly by the cock, as the hen will be starting her next brood. The young should not be separated from the parents until they are at least twenty-eight days old; it can only be good for them to be fed. They gradually learn to shell their own seeds.

A pair of Crested Canaries. This variety, also known as the German Crested, is somewhat larger than the Gloster.

CANARY BREEDING

Canaries can be bred on the colony system if sufficient room is available. This can be successful but sometimes squabbles over nesting sites will occur. Incompatibility between various birds can arise from inherited characteristics. The aviary must be very large. To many breeders, space is very valuable but very sparse.

For a long time, it has been known that a canary hen can rear chicks by herself. Thus, one cock may be used for two to four hens. When the hen has finished building the nest, the cock is introduced and left with her until she has laid at least the third egg. This can be done only when the hens are ready to nest at different times. Some experienced breeders can move the cock from hen to hen. Later, the cock must be placed out of hearing distance.

Sometimes there may be difficulties with this method; the hen may not necessarily accept a cock, which she has previously only heard singing, when he is suddenly introduced to her. One aviculturist gives a tip: "The cock is introduced at dusk. Early the following morning, at dawn, the light is switched on in the room and

A quartet of Canary eggs inside the nest.

one makes a trilling noise. In most cases, the hen will crouch and a smart cock will immediately cover her. With young, inexperienced cocks, however, success is less likely." Hens which rear their young alone should not be allowed to have as many clutches as those which are helped by the cock. Some breeders consider this method to be unnatural and state: "It is possible only because the cock is placed in a sexual emergency, and is then ready to mate with any hen." Such a method is significant if the cock is extremely good and you want as many young as possible to inherit his characteristics.

The natural method, in which birds are kept in pairs, can also have its problems. It has been reported that—fortunately rarely—cocks exist which not only do *not* feed the young but throw them out of the nest! Such birds are not suitable for breeding. It can happen that the cock or the hen will not allow the newly fledged young near the nest. In the wild, this problem would sort itself out, as there is adequate space. For similar reasons, the young can disturb the pair when they are

ready to mate again. A close watch should be kept and, if problems arise, the young can be placed in an adjacent cage, where the cock can continue to feed them through the wire. Another problem which may occur is a "real domestication torment." Many canary hens pluck the down feathers from their current brood when they are lining their nest for the next brood. In natural conditions, the birds are not confined to such a small space; the foliage and the

Opposite: Both parent birds will feed and care for the young chicks. *This page:* Parent Canary with wobbly young chicks. Note how the youngsters are trying to keep their balance.

camouflage of the feathers mean that the wild canary hen is less optically fixed on the young.

If a hen is brooding infertile eggs, one should not disturb the brood rhythm and remove the eggs too early. If the breeding does not go as planned, there is something wrong. It can be the fault of the breeder or it can be a domestication problem. "Nest building is wholly impulsive; it is not learned but is instinctive. The impulse starts as the ovaries ripen. A hen breeding for the first time can have no idea what the nest is for, as she will not 'know' that she will lay eggs, or that she will have to rear young in the nest. Exact observations have proven that young birds do not build less perfect nests than older ones, as has often been said. The stronger and better the reproductive drive is, the more perfect the nest will be. That nest building is purely instinctive and not individual enterprise is shown in that a duck only pulls in materials within reach of her beak, and never flies with materials to the nest as other birds do. And these [other birds] are further subdivided into those which carry single twigs such as pigeons, and others which pack their beaks full, as can be seen

A bevy of Canary eggs.

with every canary hen." There is, however, a learning process in canaries. One authority has written: "As with the rat . . . all nest building processes are instinctive; however, it has to learn the appropriate order of actions. Similarly, the inexperienced canary shows all the necessary actions of nest building, but must first learn to bring them to a functional result." One should therefore consider carefully before intervening. Birds which are to be shown must have leg bands fitted (as proof of one's own breeding). This is done when the youngsters are six to eight days old. These rings can be a danger as, when the hen discovers one, she may attempt to remove it (as if it were a dropping) from the nest, complete with the attached chick! This is likely to happen only during the time when the droppings are still contained within a membrane.

Red mite can be a problem and a danger to chicks when they are not controlled. Good miticides are available from your pet shop. A further problem is egg binding,which occurs time and again. The cause is often related to bad

Buff Cinnamon Yorkshire Canary.

husbandry or poor diet. It can also occur if the hen is too young. In addition, one must suspect the possible degenerative effects of domestication.

Opinions differ regarding the age at which the first molt occurs.

The first molt is a partial molt as only the down feathers are renewed. The color canary breeder must now ensure that he has got the correct diet together. Breeders of song canaries first begin to train their young cock birds after the molt (which takes eight to ten weeks). The breeder recognizes the cocks as they begin to practice. One experienced breeder states: "A few days after the young cock leaves the nest . . . he does not just sit and dream; he flicks his tail a little and quietly repeats more or less correlated notes. Such tones, though hardly to be regarded as a song, are not produced by a hen." The young cocks are placed in small cages so that, at first, they can see each other; they are later hidden from each other by screens. Here they begin their song training, with or without a "trainer" (experienced cock), whereby the breeder uses his knowledge, his experience and his intuition. Other breeders prefer to keep unusual canaries (for example, the Crested and the Border).

SOCIAL ASPECTS OF CANARY KEEPING

The beginner is lucky when his pair of canaries rears its young problem-free. If everything does not run smoothly at first attempt, do not despair. The beginner should seek advice from experienced

Young Gloster Canaries. Members of this variety leave the nest at about eighteen days of age.

breeders and it is often useful to join an avicultural society or a canary breeding club.

The behaviorist Otto Koenig describes humans as "social, territorial hunters and gatherers, acting in small groups, preferring hilly land and here preferring to live in safe, cavelike accommodation. . . . In these behavioral symptoms of animal keeping. Hunting and *gathering* from one side and striving for social *contact* on the other can be regarded as strong instincts. . . ."

Another behaviorist,Dr. Steinbacher writes: "At a time when people are increasingly alienating from each other and, in overpopulated conditions, are losing their basic contacts with nature; when technology and automation in all areas are increasing the amount of leisure time, modern man apparently seeks a reduction in stress and aggression from a satisfying activity such as animal care. Experience has shown that animal lovers suffer much less from psychological disturbances than those alienated from nature. The intensive occupation of caring for an animal will divert their worries and give them joy and inner satisfaction. This is particularly the case with regard to birds. . . ." This can be applied to keepers of a single pet bird and even more so to breeders

Breeding Canaries is a fascinating hobby, but it is one that should be given a great deal of thought before it is undertaken.

A mother Canary with her young.

who have the pleasure of seeing the young reared. He further reports on a paper from a medical journal: "In a sanatorium on the Black Sea, sleeping problems were cured with bird song." "But there are those," he continues, "who complain about early morning bird song and find it tedious. . . . But do these people complain about the much louder and more unpleasant sounds of modern technology?"

Many bird societies try to attract lay people with their bird shows and exhibitions. I, myself, experienced much interest from the public with an exhibition of nests and eggs at an information stall. Citizens of large towns were amazed at canary nests and eggs; hardly one of them had ever seen an egg other than a chicken's!

EPILOGUE

It is hard to believe that the canary will one day be forgotten. Too many people regard it as an indispensable home companion. At eight or nine years of age, children can take on the responsibility of looking after a canary, but preferably under the supervision of an older brother or sister or an adult.

Looking back into history, or at primitive peoples, shows us that animals play a part in human lives—especially pet animals. More and more people today are keeping pets or animals in the home as their only existing contact with nature. The Nobel Prize winner, Konrad Lorenz, speaks about this: "Every animal kept in the home substitutes man's contact with nature, which he has lost through civilization, and teaches him facts, the absence of which would endanger all humanity."

Unfortunately, legislation does not always consider these relationships. We are continually threatened with new difficulties with regard to home animal keeping, from the prohibition of keeping certain birds in cages (in Germany including some species which are not endangered in the wild, thus affecting the canary hybrid hobby), to taxation plans which, if they were to become reality, would mean that many enthusiasts would have to dispose of their birds.

A Red Factor Yorkshire Canary.

Index